*Brian Fewster*

# Poor Tom's Revenge

Poor Tom's Press

The poems printed here have been published in
*Poetry Review, Staple, Envoi, The Critical Survey,
Limestone Landscape, Poetry Nottingham, Poetry Monthly,
Poetry from Leicestershire, Miniwords, Exit 21,
Poetry from the Spinning Room, The Interpreter's House*
and *English in Education.*

Published by Poor Tom's Press
89a Winchester Avenue, Leicester LE3 1AY

Printed on recycled paper by Rural Press,
1a Shirley Street, Leicester LE4 5JT

*British Cataloguing-in-Publication Data*
A catalogue record for this book is available
from the British Library

ISBN 0-9543371-0-7

# Contents

# Time Out

Before you and behind you
  the long perspectives reach,
to vanish down the distance
  in ribbed and shining beach.

You seem to walk on water
  when through the midday heat
your spiralling reflection
  ripples beneath your feet.

The boats upon their hawsers
  feel a receding tide
and towards the lunar summons
  shift knocking side by side.

Locked in the sun's surveillance
  on acquiescent sand
you grip the shape of melting time
  like ice inside your hand.

# Mineshaft

The window square is turning black.
I lie upon you, drained and slack.
Already you are nowhere near.
Your fingers crawl across my back
and I am falling in your fear.
You are the cage and winding gear.

As helpless as a blinded hare,
I hear in gasps of undesire
advancing up the cellar stair
*hysterica passio* mount higher,
and wish that I were anywhere
away from here and didn't care.

But on a counterweighted wheel
this rising drops us fathoms deep,
and I must search with you surreal
infected wounds that never heal,
until exhaustion lets you creep
into my arms again and sleep.

I dream I'm in the open air,
watching the bow-wave twist and pour,
with the wind's fingers in my hair
and the momentum to ignore
from off a barren rock somewhere
the siren call of your despair.

# Black Dogs

When the transfer of property was signed
  and the possessions came to be divided,
habitual tendrils stiffly disentwined.

I ferried twenty years in cardboard boxes
  of faded magazines, abandoned books
and postcards bundled up in perished rubber,

to pore again through liver-spotted sheets
  whose names, like flies dismembered on the page,
still stir and almost coalesce to faces.

My desk remains there underneath your papers
  but I don't visit that place where I figure
no longer on the register of electors.

Those that we might have been hungrily watch us
  crumble and waste the lives they might have had.
See how they stretch to lick our sticky fingers!

# What We Don't Know

*In memory of Annie, the wife of W K Stephenson*
*of Settle, who died the 24th October 1850.*
*Also of Arthur their son, who died the 7th day*
*of November 1850, aged 19 days*
*Tombstone in Settle Churchyard*

You read your body's bloodless auguries:
  promise of life or economic threat,
extending a line, starting a new story
  or wrapping you more tightly in a net.

Was it your first confinement or your tenth?
  The epitaph omits how old you were
and whether you were kind and quick to laugh
  and with what hope or fear you felt him stir.

Carrying him the best part of a year
  you must have thought about him every day.
You knew that being pregnant often meant
  nine months of work screwed up and thrown away.

Your husband's dates are not recorded here.
  We don't know how much time he had for grief,
whether the baby might have struggled through
  or if the nineteenth day brought sour relief.

Only the mathematics are exact,
  a trap for casual connoisseurs of dates
to spring a sudden blurring of the eyes
  and a blind look to where the future waits.

# Territory

*another dead cat poem*

As a conservative old man
to whom your needs and rights were one
   (regular meals at decent times
digested slowly in the sun)

by eight o'clock you'd wait no more
but knock outright with blunted paw
   in just rebuke of morning sloth
like any human at the door.

You knew the limits of your sway
and walked them several times a day
   in grim patrol along the wall
to warn all trespassers away

but seldom ventured into what
lay past our vegetable plot
   until you crossed the boundary
between what is and what is not,

where the unformed and obsolete
in unimagined numbers beat
   against the edge of entity
with insubstantial wings and feet.

Though one or two may flicker through
the rustling throng and for a few
   beleaguered moments occupy
substantial form, as me or you,

once out there's no return, so when
at eight o'clock we hear a thin
   persistent scratching on the door
we can't come down and let you in.

# Home

Through broken monuments and scaffolding
 I drive my body like a builder's crane.
Each limb's a weight to lift, a load to swing.
  The force of will controls the fact of pain.
The television prattles on unheard.
  Distraction claws and corrugates the page,
while fading sensibilities are stirred
  by archive footage blipped and cracked with age.

The fear of shame conceals the face of fear.
  All movement's plotted.  Always at my back
the brisk impatient "Come along then, dear".
  I've known enough of love to know its lack.
Marooned in plush velour and polished chrome.
Lost in the heart of brightness.  Far from home.

# The Committee

There's one in nursery teaching
  and one in holy orders,
and others have the silhouettes
  of police or prison warders.

It isn't hard to eavesdrop
  on their deliberation,
where measured praise is condiment
  to overall damnation.

With never-failing patience,
  they sit in constant session.
The power of absolution
  is not in their possession.

They take my deposition
  concerning each depravity
through microphones implanted
  inside the cranial cavity.

At night they're hyperactive,
  with polymorphic faces,
to rubberneck and nose about
  the dark secluded places.

Negotiating keyholes
  as easily as vapour,
they crawl through my unconsciousness
  like sparks on smouldering paper,

and while my sleeping system
  flies blind on automatic,
directions lost for routes I've crossed
  still crackle through the static.

# I'd Like to Save the World, but...

I wish I could attend your demonstrations:
  although my diary's jam-packed every day
I care about the coming generations.
  Believe me, friend, I'm with you all the way.

Each year the price of indecision rises.
  I'd like to give your candidate my vote
but my financial analyst advises
  that now is not the time to rock the boat.

Your arguments present the issue starkly
  and, while the wind caresses it with sleet,
I'm gazing on the double glazing darkly.
  The curtain stirs and shivers in the heat.

The cityscape beyond is white and sheeny,
  with supplicants in an amorphous mass.
They swirl about like gin in my martini
  and press their faces up against the glass,

but since I am no hero, saint or wizard
  I take my comfort while the rafters burn.
Outside, the snowstorm strengthens to a blizzard
  that melts and slides upon my warm concern.

# Poor Tom's Revenge

*With a heart of furious fancies*
*Whereof I am commander,*
*    With a burning spear and a horse of air*
*To the wilderness I wander.*
                    *Tom o' Bedlam*

Let others find their answers
in Kant or Aristotle.
  A hole at night's my guiding light;
my comfort's in this bottle.

I cower in smashed apartments
and weed-infested craters
  while blundering by, ten storeys high,
rampage the wealth-creators.

All through the bitter winter
I watch from Cardboard City
  how graciously the pharisee
doles out his pence and pity.

But when the fit's upon me
through crowds I bawl my lungs out.
  With fisted stones I batter phones
and tear their drivelling tongues out.

I snap the roadside saplings
with effortless disdain.
  Unlucky flies must recognise
in me their God of Pain.

With my enormous shadow
I stun the politicians.
  Their matchbox town I trample down
and all their wise ambitions.

# Stop-Frame Sequence

Flickering behind the railings over the traffic
the boy staggers, cradling the concrete block,
heaves its weight on to the barrier,
opens his mouth soundlessly into the wind
and slowly spreads his arms to let it topple.

Between the motorway bridge and the fast lane
the huge fragment hangs like a meteorite,
displaying irregularities as it turns.

Cut to side view of traffic under the bridge
through the projected point of intersection
towards which the missile now jumps frame by frame
until its flint point meets resistant metal
that dimples initially like skin on water
but relaxes and tears as the insistent visitor
forces its way in.  The radio is playing jazz,
the driver improvising a scat accompaniment

which is observed by the boy from his small Olympus,
as his heart begins to beat with elated horror
at such a bodying forth of imagination
by actors of flesh and blood, steel and stone.

# Hard Man

Inscrutable in mirrored shades,
  I broadcast hatred hot and strong.
It rains on all of your parades.
  No fucker looks at me for long.

I'm wise to what you're playing at
  with scowls and sneers when safe behind
and whispering ways to bell the cat.
  What's out of sight is out of mind.

I ride the element of power
  as native as the shark at sea.
It buoys me up while hour by hour
  the steady slipstream swims with me,

creating space for me to swim
  through looks deflected left and right,
dependent on my passing whim
  and subject to my appetite.

# Waiting

All the windows gape like doors on a baker's oven.
  Nothing anywhere moves with any sense of urgency
except the birds, lifting and fanning in one action.

Trees pose with formal stiffness for the lightning flash,
  a leaf or two vibrating if you watch carefully,
while the unhurried sky gets its equipment together,

trowelling into place a massive baroque cloudbank,
  draped and curlicued, its swollen immodest contours
ochrish like wet plaster, ice-creamy along the edges,

but the audience begins to sense that it isn't going to happen:
  only the evening traffic and the next trainload of rubble
thundering towards the embankment with tired resignation.

# Geography Lesson

Like arctic spawn conceived in light
we no more comprehend the night
than mountain streams, whose waters spill
from stone to stone, can run uphill.

But water that returns as rain
replenishes the stream again
and light on shadow, sun in space,
so follow their unhurried pace

that while the summer seems to stay
the pole drifts darkward day by day.


# Tickertape

All hearts hammer tickertape time.
                                At last
comes the big black motorcade, gliding past
through an incandescence of drifting snow
that litters the boulevard below
our waving arms and wild white faces
with dots
            and crosses
                        and empty spaces.

*No one else has yet attempted a modern verse paraphrase of this recently-discovered fragment of Chaucer's* Prologue, *and the parallel version on the right is therefore offered with all due modesty as a useful aid to appreciation until something better comes along. I have deliberately not gone for a literal translation, but tried to transpose it into a more contemporary idiom, and if anyone feels that I've taken too many liberties I can only plead, with Chaucer, that "my wit is short, ye may wel understonde".*

## The Maker

Ther was a maker, riche in blood and coler,
A cherl y-boren, yet a lerned scholer,
For him was lever have in-side his heed
Twenty bokes, burning blak and reed
Than 'Neigheboures' or 'Coronacioun Strete'.[1]                     5
He seyde ryming hadde y-growen effete
In dogerel y-goon from bad to wers,
But he wolde put a fyr-werke up its ers.
He was nat lik a hounde withinne a stalle
For wisdome wolde he gladly teche to al,                            10
But as he waxed hye in passioun
And rhetorice and diffinicioun
On scriveynes that were other deef or blinde
Some thoughte that he hadde y-loste his minde.
His drye lippes worched while his eyne,                             15
As that some incubus dide him distreyne,
Semed to seke a twisting in the aire,
Al swete and savourous, that was nat ther.[2]

[1] *These are thought to be references to scurrilous popular ballads.*
[2] *The passage has not been adequately explained. Dr Schmidt has observed that the maker shows signs of nicotine withdrawal, but most scholars regard this as implausible two centuries before our country's introduction to the doubtful pleasures of tobacco.*

# The Poet

There was a poet rich in blood and choler,
For he was both iconoclast and scholar,
And – though a connoisseur of curious data,
A juxtaposer and a tesselater,
A reinterpreter and rearranger –
He was not like a mongrel in a manger,
But shared his wisdom with the common crowd.
"*Down with élitist verse!*" he'd cry aloud.
"*Destroy the mould! We've got to make it new,*
*As Ezra said in 1322.*
*Away with cliché, custom, commonsense!*" [1]
But as his eloquence grew more intense
Some cynics said the sage had lost his grip,
Observing how his fingers sought his lip
And how he sucked his teeth, then heaved a sigh –
While all the time his agitated eye
Seemed haunted by a twisting in the air,
A fragrant effluence that wasn't there.

---

[1] *This section includes perhaps the most extreme of the liberties I have taken. The doctrine of permanent revolution may not have been invented in the fourteenth century, but let us not forget that Chaucer was a contemporary of Wat Tyler and John Ball.*

# Re-Reading Auden

1

This lank-haired, pasty-faced young busker
isn't the act I came prepared for:
gauche, intense, a taker of risks
of a precocious disproportion,
raw, lacking in circumspection,
unpredictable in direction.

Travelling through my practised patter
(left hand, right hand, find the lady)
for an audience of two or three
idlers and children at the market's edge,
I envy each inelegant gesture
with which a dead man stamps his future.

2

We live like you in a low dishonest decade.
The new age never existed except in the mind
(though all things exist there).  Idols are clay-footed
and slow plodding's the only locomotion.
The dream I had that the lean years would outlast me
edges into the light.  This fin-de-siècle
brings the return of nightmares thought to be over,
where cleanliness is next to inhumanity,
and the sins of the fathers (generations ago
released like spores into the atmosphere)
teach the lessons of history to ignorant children.

Civic woodcutters are always ready
to see the wolf in the bedridden old woman,
and the words you spoke at the edge of the dark forest
are truer and more impossible than ever:
collectively we must love one another or die.

3

Every year at Hallowe'en
mythic monsters mop and preen.
Some require continually
that savage anonymity.

When the children slipped their traces,
metamorphosed to master races,
innocent and knowing eyes
with habitual surprise
witnessed from a crumpled face
corruption of the human race.

Every generation finds
monstrous masks for little minds.
In the vaults of superstition
ancient shapes take definition.
Little Darlings pant beneath
Tinkerbells with pointed teeth.
Symbols of annihilation
in iconic celebration
strut in Tinkertown parades.
Though it's more than two decades
since the housewife History
having squeezed your poetry
threw the human pith away
we can use those eyes today.

# Earth-Mother to Oedipus

I smelt familiar blood about that hand
  whose grip confirmed your title to the crown,
but being your possession, on demand
  obediently I laid my body down.

You never did distinguish love from rape
  before the plague informed you what you'd done.
Imprisoned in an act with no escape,
  You've fathered where you were conceived, my son:

forbidden knowledge, gained without seduction,
  since heroes need no argument but force;
and now, my child, my lover, my destruction,
  negotiate alone your blind remorse.

# Cassandra

An eye for now and one for what's to be
define in depth a vision none believes.
When both are open how it hurts to see

the peerless Hector buckling on his greaves!
Like an infection on her skin she feels
the prickling of the prophecy, perceives

what time's forbearance from the rest conceals:
that glow of power and virtue and desire
flayed raw behind Achilles' chariot wheels.

She turns at night upon a funeral pyre
and wakes to meet the certainties she dreads,
but when she tries to warn of how the fire

will blacken shambled streets and blood-soaked beds,
or share the consequential grief and pain,
the corpses smile and tap their bloated heads

in mimic sympathy: "She's off again!"

# The Seven Deadly Sins

## 1. Pride

He knows the moving spirits, meets them all
  at pleasant soirées on his private yacht.
His portrait's hanging on the panelled wall.
  He's in *Who's Who* and understands what's what.
His Daimler sports a custom registration.
  His shirts are monogrammed with his initials.
The nuts and bolts of each deliberation
  are screwed in place by diligent officials.

He is a sun with satellites that live
to pivot on the weight of what he wants
  with flattery at every orifice.
He dines at night in mirrored restaurants
and has by day his own executive
  white marble privacy in which to piss.

## 2. Hate

*The younger generation's gone to pot:*
  *we're breeding scruffs, degenerates and yobs.*
*The taxman gobbles everything we've got*
  *and foreigners are filling all our jobs.*
*The legal system's run by bleeding hearts.*
  *The social workers haven't got a clue.*
*There's subsidised subversion in the arts*
  *that rots our moral fibre through and through.*

*No wonder England's going down the drain*
  *now money's poured away on foreign aid*
*and prison's fun and scroungers sip champagne*
  *and no one dares to call a spade a spade.*
  *Scores will be settled and the interest paid*
*when decent people crack the whip again.*

# The Seven Deadly Sins

## 3. Lust

Although his one ambition is to find
   that moment when endurance and delay
have blotted out all vestiges of mind,
   he's not uncultivated in his way.
His well-thumbed books fall open at the place
   where heroine succumbs at last to hero.
He moves towards his prey with practised grace,
   humming the rhythm of Ravel's *Bolero* –
scanning the body first, and then the face
   to quantify the eyes for depth of black.
He likes the way Picasso twisted space
and let erotic elements push forth
   uncluttered by the usual bric-a-brac.

His compass needle always points to north.

## 4. Envy

*Cold Turkey Cure for Politician's Wife –*
  *How Controversial Scribe went Barking Mad –*
*Ex-Beauty Queen Declares she's Tired Of Life –*
  *Pop Millionaire Neglects his Poor Old Dad –*
*Spectacular Demise of Well-Loved Clown –*
  *Mistress Spills All – Exclusive Revelation –*
*Crusader Photographed with Trousers Down*
  and *schadenfreude* unifies the nation.

C tells of D's proclivities in bed –
  confides in tears that he and she are through.
Ex claims estate in settlement from Z ...
  (what sweet anticipation swells in you
as lion's mouth meets lion-tamer's head)
and – deary me! – Lord W is dead!

# The Seven Deadly Sins

## 5.  Avarice

*The system needs incentives, and must pay*
  *the market rate for managerial skill.*
*No matter what the Jeremiahs say,*
  *the profit's there to take if we've the will*
*to trim the fat and junk the featherbeds:*
  *by vigilant outsourcing and downsizing*
*we've cut the wage-related overheads*
  *and, thanks to us, the dividends are rising.*

*Our corporate commitment shows its strength*
  *in all industrial negotiations –*
*where we hold kings and aces, and at length*
  *the workforce must scale down its expectations.*
*It knows the market, in this day and age,*
*is what dictates an economic wage.*

## 6. Gluttony

Mammoth for starters, charcoaled medium rare,
  followed by aurochs in a herbal dressing
and *crudités des forêts de la terre*
  garnished with oil a million years in pressing.
From stuffed auk, battered dodo, bison steak
  to wallaby and passenger-pigeon pie,
the gourmet-sacrifices crowd to slake
  this craving they can never satisfy.

By now he's been at table all day long
  and midnight nears, but still the helpings fail
to satiate an appetite so strong.
  The waiter's lined up elephant and whale
and then, as a reward for such persistence,
the final course – his own obese existence.

# The Seven Deadly Sins

## 7. Sloth

There are so many urgent things to do,
  the sooner he can start on them the better.
He lounges on his back and counts them through:
  the ailing relative who'd love a letter,
the cheque he'd meant to write for each good cause –
  they link to load his limbs down with a fetter
of unmet deadlines and unmanaged chores.
  Procrastinator, dilettante, debtor,
he hears the whisper of descending sand
  that grain by grain reminds him life is real
and tangible and trickles through his hand.
  He'd quickly set his shoulder to the wheel
once extricated from this bed of thorns.

Tears crawl along his temples while he yawns.

# Vicisti

*after Swinburne*

You've mastered us all, market forces.
  The world has grown grey with your breath.
As strict as the stars in their courses
  that twinkle disaster and death,

you rule that our old ways are ended,
  that justice is balanced on sheets,
tradition and trust are suspended
  and charity begs on the streets.

We must sail where the sirens are calling
  across the impersonal flood:
*"Tomorrow in futures is falling,*
  *get out while the going is good."*

So peasants in faraway places
  go empty and cold in their bones
when hard-eyed young men with red braces
  shout numbers down portable phones.

# Arms and the Man

It gives me pleasure, underneath
   this heading, to present a prize
to you, Sir Worldly Wisdom-Teeth,
   for *Services to Enterprise.*

You've often praised the soldier's creed
   because of its ability
to crush the forces that impede
   political stability.

In global commerce you maintain
   the scope of Mephistopheles
and feed directly from the vein
   as sweetly as *anopheles*

until replete with interest,
   in your black BMW
encapsulated and caressed.
   No doubts or debits trouble you

but (though compassion's not what you'd
   invest your reputation in)
you're sometimes in the giving mood,
   and send a small donation in.

The damaged and untimely dead
   you keep the windows shuttered on
while grafting for your daily bread.
   You know which side it's buttered on.

# Ballade of Intuitive Statesmanship

A policy's considered sound
  that with insouciant élan
juggles the dollar and the pound.
  A year ahead's the most we plan.
  At rendezvous of shit and fan
with any luck we'll be elsewhere
  and crossing bridges one by one
seems like a sensible idea.

Veterans of the game have found
  it pays where proletarian
and bourgeois moralists abound
  to play the strict Victorian;
  but don't be over-puritan
if spreading palm and bending ear
  on sinner and on publican
seems like a sensible idea.

So foot it featly on the ground,
  and wave away utopian
dreams of dispersing wealth around
  beyond this elegant pavane.
  Those of another class or clan
deserve suspicion, scorn and fear:
  man's inhumanity to man
seems like a sensible idea.

*ENVOI*

Prince, while the world's attention span
  keeps on contracting year by year,
to get away with what we can
  seems like a sensible idea.

# Sixpenny Song

Long light of afternoon
  lies on the grass.
Black birds and brown birds
  pass and re-pass.

Two-thirds a natural span
  having spun by
(eight-and-forty black years
  baked in a pic)

living room is painted,
  all but a wedge,
waiting for the pie chart
  to meet edge to edge.

As the pie closes
  birds begin to sing.
Afternoon is brim full
  of sweet jargoning.

# Banshee

*Oh why* the ripple down the road,
  the ululating cry
that vehicles in lapse of haste
  huddle to let go by,
  *oh why oh why oh why?*

*Oh who* is all the panic for,
  the fierce pulsating blue
that wills a windowless white box
  imperiously through,
  *oh who oh who oh who?*

*Oh where* is this wild panoply
  transporting one in there?
out of the unpredictable
  undemarcated air,
  *oh where oh where oh where?*

*Away* from time and tenderness
  and teacups on a tray,
the improvised extravagance
  of each recovered day,
  *away away away.*

*O you* that stand irresolute,
  uncertain what to do
with this black-bordered envelope
  or whom to post it to:
  *o you o you o you.*

# Wish You Were Here

Since dawn we've all been passengers together,
  cool intimates of sound and sight and scent
by chance enrolment on this expedition
  across a huge and ill-mapped continent.

We've found at every halt the dialect strange,
  the population different in physique,
while unremitting in its disposition
  to misinterpret our attempts to speak.

But the engine has stood still all afternoon.
  Picture me scribbling this communication
from the metropolis of Midlife-Crisis
  in a refreshment room close to the station

before the long climb into the hills,
  with their increasingly uncouth facilities,
inclement weather and indifferent service,
  exacerbates our urban sensibilities.

No one is in a hurry to continue,
  but soon the mutinous and the resigned
will take up their reserved accommodation
  and see the lighted platform slide behind,

until their pale reflections in the windows
  are all that's left to move the imagination
from rosary-clicks and mantras of great wheels
  ticking off time towards its destination.